Graham-isms

Thoughts That Almost Crossed My Mind

೧೦——೧೩

"Nothing is so useless as a general maxim."
Thomas Macaulay
(1800–1859)

Rev. Dr. J. Donald Graham

Graham-isms
Thoughts That Almost Crossed My Mind

Copyright ©2016 J. Donald Graham
ALL RIGHTS RESERVED

First Printing – September 2016

ISBN: 978-0-9968933-2-9 *(paperback)*

NO PART OF THIS BOOK MAY BE REPRODUCED IN ANY FORM, BY PHOTOCOPYING OR BY AN ELECTRONIC OR MECHANICAL MEANS, INCLUDING INFORMATION STORAGE OR RETRIEVAL SYSTEMS, WITHOUT PERMISSION IN WRITING FROM THE COPYRIGHT OWNER/AUTHOR.

Printed in the United States of America on acid-free paper.

Published by Mosaic Design Book Publishers
Dearborn, Michigan USA

0 1 2 3 4 5 6 7 8 9

*To my daughter Suzanne
who has always been a delight to me.*

Preface

When I was teaching at Berea College, I would overhear my students quote me and add, "That's a Graham-ism." I didn't remember using that term myself, but I did like to write brief sayings.

I put my sayings on bookmarks and sold them in the craft shop that my wife, daughter, and I owned on the college square. I'm thankful to the customers who bought the bookmarks, and several of them encouraged me to put them in a book. One customer even drew a cover for the book. It pictured a road because he liked the Robert Frost poem "I took the road less traveled…" to which I had added, "And did I get lost!"

So, here are some of my sayings in book form for better or worse (maybe both).

J. Donald Graham
Berea, Kentucky
June 22, 2016

Be understanding when life is ambiguous,
paradoxical, and full of hyperbole.

I placed my one and only lottery ticket in my Bible
next to the passage that reads,
"Blessed are the poor."

What happens when you don't understand
the theory or its practice?

☙

Why can't I be an exception?

The trouble with the gods is that
they are always made in our image.

I didn't dodge the draft. The draft dodged me.

☙

The ultimate test of a sense of humor
is the ability to laugh at your self.

Be sure to get the last laugh
and also make sure it's on you.

If you can laugh at yourself,
you have a real sense of humor.

☙

Historians say that history doesn't repeat itself.
It looks to me as if that is all it does.
(If it doesn't, there are a lot of similarities.)

Our only hope is that God's love is unconditional.

They say that when you bring a cat into the house,
you bring in a little wildness.
(That goes for children, too!)

☙

The twentieth century:
God, what a catastrophe for untold millions!

The only thing winter needs is a good death.

If you had to choose, it's better to be out of faith and hope
than to be out of love.

☙

We are fighting genetics as well as the environment,
and we're losing.

Nature can turn on you!
Nature curses as well as blesses.
(And sometimes at the same time.)

Political statements should not be made in the
White House Rose Garden; it's bad for the roses.

❧

A done deal may be good for business,
but it's always bad English.

If you want life to be good to you, be good to it.

Don't ask whether or not life has been good to you.
Rather ask whether or not you have been good to life.

❧

You know the state of American medicine
when the only doctor who will make
a house call is Dr. Kevorkian.

Carefree is not an option.

I go back to the country
where the world is still recognizable.

❧

We avoid calling a spade a spade by euphemisms.
Euphemisms are also the same as denials.

Sometimes life is so bad
we have to deal with it euphemistically.

We can't shield reality with euphemisms.

☯

When we start getting it altogether
is about the time we start falling apart.

I think I did graduate work at Slip-Shod University.

The symbolic color of teaching is blue,
and that is appropriate because blue is
the color of the horizon, and
teachers are always teaching toward it.

☯

The way to keep from being
an unhappy camper is not to go to camp.

One thing about getting old is
everybody looks familiar.

Freud wrote a book entitled
Civilization & Its Discontents.
Can you imagine the discontents without civilization?

☯

Do you ever feel like your schedule is on a two-hour delay?

Many of the old would not want
to be young again because they can't imagine
youth without all of its foolishness.

Either one — poverty or riches — is hard to handle.

☙

Friends are those who listen to your stories
over and over again but never let on
they have heard them all before.

The reason my ship didn't come in
was that I was landlocked.

If you want your ship to come in,
move to the shore.

☙

Money and a spring snow
don't stay around very long.

I wish winter would pay more attention
to the vernal equinox.

The vernal equinox doesn't mean a thing
to Old Man Winter.

☙

I'm still blown away by the mystery of it all.

All things lead to profundity,
then on to mystery.

On the seesaw of life,
get on the short end of the plank.

☯

The reason they call it higher education is
that it is out of reach for many people.

The one thing that Americans have
in common with people all over the world
is the desire for American money.

A rose garden was not promised
but neither was a thicket.

☯

God must have a difficult time listening
to prayers for opposite things.

I never knew money because
I never had enough to get acquainted.

If you can't get back to Square 1,
at least get back to Square 2.

☯

I'm a born again and again and again,
world without end kind of Christian.

The trouble with a large family is
that in order to have a reunion, you have to
contact the convention bureau.

Today is the last day of my
new beginning tomorrow.

ஐ

Why does time these days seem
to be on FAST FORWARD?

You can tell you're getting older
when you start telling it like it was.

If all the world's a stage and
we're merely players, then what's the play?

ஐ

Colleges and universities are like Humpty-Dumpties.
They take you apart, but all the professors and
administrators can't put you back together again.

If you cleaned out a woman's purse,
you could almost pay off the mortgage.

You are supposed to wear your learning lightly,
but I had a teacher who wore it heavily,
and did she ever bear down on us!

☯

Religion is judged by how it treats God and people.

Eternity is not endless time.
It is the absence of time,
lest we take our alarm clocks to heaven.

Can you explain how love can make you
crazy and sane at the same time?

☯

I'm not as interested in the Big Bang
as I am in who set it off.
(But that's theology.)

No miracles of the Bible,
made an old person young again,
and that should tell us something.

A branch of psychology has become
theology in the sense that it tries to
explain the spiritual.

☯

Keep in the currents of life.

Of all the secrets of life, love is the greatest.

Baseball used to be the American pastime.
Now it's American greed-time.

ಉ

The room of grief is empty at first,
but then it can be filled with joyous memories.

Memory Lane is to go down a one-way street.

The hardest thing is to run
your own business.
The easiest thing is to tell someone else
how to run theirs.

ಉ

You really have to work hard at being
a disbeliever after hearing Mozart.

"They also serve who only stand and wait."
John Milton

Know the difference between being and doing,
and when being is doing.

ಉ

When it comes to living,
some people are just looking.

If you had more fun growing up
than you did as a grown up,
keep growing up.

Practice being an ordinary person, and
your friends will find you extraordinary.

℘

You spend the first half of life
climbing the ladder of sophistication,
and the last half climbing back down.

Always start with life's mystery,
And life's practicalities will find
their rightful place. *(Maybe.)*

The wisest among us know which questions
have answers and which ones don't.

℘

Why is it when we're lost,
we're never close to home?

If you can't afford to,
or can't afford not to,
either way, you come up short.

We may think there are God-forsaken places,
but there're not.

☯

A lot of people need to downsize their lives.
(And I'm not talking about their weight.)

There are no such things as American aristocrats.
There are just those who think they are.

The only aristocracy in America
is the aristocracy of character.

☯

On my gravestone, put:
S OMEHOW HE MUDDLED THROUGH THE MYSTERY.

When people complain about never going anywhere,
they forget their yearly voyage around the sun.

If you get the short end of the stick,
at least you can make toothpicks.

☯

Economic reckoning comes to nations
as well as to individuals.

The goal of growing up is maturity.
or it should be.

Affluence may be the worst thing
that could happen to a person or a society.

༶

We think we can handle riches, but it always ends up
the other way around: riches handle us.

Shun riches like the plague.

Occasionally pray for failure
so that you may learn to handle success.

༶

I took the road less traveled.
and did I get lost!
(apologies to Robert Frost)

Awake each day to love,
laughter, music, and dancing.
(If you can work them in.)

May the joys of your hellos
overcome the griefs of your goodbyes.

༶

See to it that the grass is greener on your side.

When money talks,
its words are not suitable for delicate ears.

We elect our politicians to do a job for us,
not on us.

☯

Every time you get ready to start living,
something happens,
so make what happens your living.

If the universe was made to impress us,
it worked!

If we dared to show off like spring and autumn,
we would be called monumental egotists.

☯

As long as we are shocked by corruption and scandal,
we're safe, for it's when we fail to be shocked
that we're in danger.

If we humans knew in depth what we hold in common,
there could be no serious divisions among us.

Life causes you to keep taking
incompletes in the university of hard knocks.

☯

I have the uneasy feeling that
I'm not going to fit into the twenty-first century
any better than I fitted into the twentieth.

Those who live on the edge are not in danger only of falling
off but also of being pushed.

No situation lasts forever—good or bad.

☙

I don't know why they call them universities.
They should call them Diversities.

I looked up from a busy life and
discovered that I was old.

How much higher is higher education going to go?
It broke me.

☙

I can't define common sense, but I know it when I see it.

What about the people who want to live and can't,
and those who can won't?

All I needed to know
I learned in kindergarten is
all right for those who didn't flunk kindergarten.
(Apologies to Robert Fulghum)

☯

Stretching our minds should not bend us out of shape.

You're not as old as you feel.
You're as old as you're old.

Life seems to get stranger and stranger
the longer we live.

☯

We all wonder if after death we will be or not be,
yet few wonder where we were before we be'd.

Neurotic is sometimes mistaken as exotic.

We sometimes pass others like clouds racing to a storm.

☯

Seek contentment.
It lasts longer than happiness.

As long as there is a cat in the house,
a home is not free.

They're up in Washington being big shots
While we are down here being little shots.
The country would be better off if we reversed it.
(At least, we'd know who's doing the shooting.)

Hope that when you're gone,
they will do a reassessment.

Despair has no foundation to build on
while hope gives you a handle to hold on to.

I'll tell you what I want along with a pacemaker:
a reset button.

☙

My Waldon Pond was on Peachbloom Hill Lane.

My Waldon Pond is within me.

I'm confused. Which is better,
the window of opportunity
or opportunity knocking at the door?

☙

I've never heard of someone
losing a needle in a haystack.
Have you?

I'm an absolutist, relatively speaking.

Who says you can't stand in the way of progress?

☙

Don't push the envelope; open it!

If capitalism is not based on the love of money,
it is, at least, based on a deep affection for it.

If someone says he can't say enough
good things about you, ask him to try.

☯

If early to bed and early to rise
makes one healthy, wealthy, and wise,
what does *The Tonight Show* do for you?

They say that age is just a number, and
I believe it because it's done a number on me.

Look on the absurdity side of life
and you'll make it through.

☯

The bottom line and I walked hand in hand
for years until it pushed me off the cliff.
Such is the fickleness of the bottom line.

Be thankful that
Fame and Fortune passed you by.

When Jesus, in Luke's gospel, said from the cross,
"Father, forgive them. They know not what they're doing,"
that got us all off the hook.
*(Our inhumanity and insanity was laid
to ignorance and not to our total depravity.)*

※

God has a way of throwing us back to the beginning,
lest we become too proud of our so-called advancement.

I don't play the lottery.
Life is lottery enough for me.

Civilization is our distraction from our lost-ness.

※

No one could have predicted
how our lives would turn out.
For some, a great ride, and for others a train wreck.

I have a hard time believing in a hell in the afterlife,
But I sure as hell believe in hell in this life.

I find that C. S. Lewis was right
when he said that grief and fear are similar.

※

My knowledge of history is anecdotal:
(A story here, a story there.)
I can't figure out how the whole thing goes.

We are all opinionated, but the question is:
Can we change our opinions?
We had better.

One thing that never changes is
human nature, and that's the one thing
that needs changing.
(for the better, that is!)

❧

Just say he lived and loved the mystery of the universe.
(My God, what are we doing here, anyway?)

Mad ain't got you nothing but trouble.

A philosopher said that life is absurd,
but I still think it's kind of cute.

❧

The problems of the world will not be solved
around conference tables but around an altar.
(If they can be solved at all.)

When we were young, time was slow;
now that we are older, time is anything but slow.

Politics is like the weather.
Everyone talks about it,
but no one does anything about it.
(I'm talking about the voters.)

❦

I came to my thirst for knowledge late,
and then it was too late.

I'm a recovering cynic,
but lately I've fallen off the wagon.

I hungered for knowledge, but
I had a bad digestive system.

❦

We usually find an outlook
that matches our emotional makeup.

A lot of so-called worship is more suited
to the rock concert than it is to the church.

If the problem of evil is hard to answer,
what about the problem of good?

❦

If the immensity of the universe was
God's way of astounding us, He succeeded.

A dilemma of freedom is recognizing it in
someone who would deny it to you.

Sex reveals more than our nakedness.

☙

At best, life is a mixed bag,
and it's meaning is not in the mixture
but in how we carry it.

What if the strings of your heart get tangled up?
(It is like being unstrung.)

Mired in the morass of the mystery,
I could hardly extricate myself to face the
practicalities of life.

☙

The business of thinking outside the box
depends on how big the box is.
(and what's outside)

The problem with infinity
is that we approach it with "finity."

You know you are getting old
when historical events are mentioned and
you have lived through them.

☙

I wanted to downsize when it occurred
to me that I had never been upsized.

If you can find pleasure in little things,
you'll always be happy
for life is mostly made up of little things.

The more the questions,
the fewer the answers.

☙

What is more important:
to know where you're going
or to know where you've been?
(Why not both?)

I never forgot where I came from, but I tried.

We're in trouble when imitation
can look more real than real.

☙

Have you noticed that those who deny the existence
of God are as preoccupied with His
non-existence as believers are in
His existence?

I thought that political correctness
was just trying to be polite.

In the university of hard knocks,
we never get out of the freshman class.
And we can't drop out, either.

※

Does a fond farewell mean
you're glad they're leaving?

For a reader, life is never boring.

Friendship is hard to explain
but not hard to experience.

※

Restraint not censorship

Money doesn't talk. It screams.

I got above my raising. My mother saw to it.

※

I wonder about "world class"
for fear that it might have more
world than class.

Be sure to know which direction
the crowd is going
or you may fall off a cliff.

In business,
I paid no attention to the bottom line.
(By the way, I'm not in business anymore.)

❧

Old age is not measured in years alone
but in how many times you've told
the same story over and over again.

Shouldn't we be intolerant of intolerance?

From dust we came and to dust we shall return
leaves a lot to be desired.

❧

Freedom is absolute but not in this world.

Forgiving is not condoning.

Life allows no retakes.
(That's what forgiveness is for.)

❧

The light at the end of my tunnel
suffered a cave-in.

If atheists worship anything,
let them worship the mystery of our existence
and the existence of worlds.

If you're not confused,
you don't understand the question.

❧

The only thing that doesn't change is change.
It just keeps rolling along.

I love people.
It's the individual that I have trouble with.

Power roughs you up.
Love picks you up.

❧

The disintegration of civilization
is in direct proportion to the amount of litter.
Save civilization.
Don't litter!

What is more beautiful to see
than the delight in a child's eyes?

The only scandal preachers should be involved in
is the scandal of the gospel.

☯

Do you think God is fine-tuning the universe,
and we're causing all the static?

Most of us are destined to observe history,
not to make it.
(Either way, it's quite a show!)

When you are eyeball to eyeball with despair,
don't be the first to blink.

☯

When you are too full of yourself,
look up at the stars.
(Astronomy has cured many an ego.)

The biggest mistake a society or an individual
can make is to believe it is value-free.

We should love our country enough
to confront its faults.

☯

"Fine" is one of the best words in the language.
It almost rivals "beautiful."

Would nature spoil us if
we had only spring and fall?

A rising tide doesn't lift all boats.
Some of them sink.

☯

Our reason is like a small boat
battered by a storm of emotion.

Many chase the almighty dollar
while saints chase the Almighty.

In life, we're always an apprentice or a novice.

☯

If it's not broke, don't fix it.
But you'd better keep it tuned.

God is too big a concept for science to handle.
It doesn't have the tools.

Doubt is not all bad.

☯

There is nothing like getting old to change
your perspective *(and everything else)*.

When the stock market has a correction,
I have a conniption.

At the least,
surround yourself with great friends,
great ideas, great music, great art,
great hope, and a great love.

☯

I thought getting old
was what happened to other people.

I didn't realize that inside every old person
was a young person. If I had, I would have
stopped to play with them.

Life is like running a gamut!

☯

We try to freeze time, but it always melts.

Life is mostly poetry: some sad, some glad.

When I tried to get rid of clutter,
I found I had gotten rid of my life.

☯

What a tyrant the majority can be.

When do I graduate from the
University of Hard Knocks?

You have to stare unhappiness down.

ಬ

Declare yourself a roaring success
and get on with your life.

Sign a peace treaty with yourself
or it will declare war on you.

Don't look up from a busy life
and find it has passed you by.

ಬ

Henry David Thoreau didn't want to come
to the end of his life
and discover that he had not lived.
I just don't want to come to the end of my life.
Period.

Procrastination is God's gift to the confused.

It's all right to be opinionated
as long as you can change your opinions.

ಬ

If everyone has their price,
make yours so high that no one could pay it.

A life of ease is hard on a person.

As long as we're here, why not look around?

୭

Instead of passing each other
like ships in the night,
we're more likely to collide.

Isn't life lived with the myths we choose,
or maybe it's a myth-understanding.

Tell them my timing was off.

୭

You can't build anything on despair, only hope.

Be thirsty for knowledge but hungry for wisdom.

Who says you can't stand in the way of progress?
I did.

୭

If the early bird gets the worm,
why doesn't he get sick?

When God closes the door and
doesn't open a window,
you're in big trouble.

If you ever tell someone to "get a life,"
please have the courtesy to show him
where he can find it.

༄

A philosopher tries to find the meaning of things,
and a theologian tries to find God as
the meaning of things.

A poet makes words dance.

Take others seriously but not yourself so much.

༄

We have all these labor-saving devices,
yet we labor more than ever.
(I'm tired, aren't you?)

If life would just hold still,
I think I could get a good picture.

To follow the crowd is not to know
where you're going.

༄

If you get the cart before the horse,
You have to be very creative to get it going.

If I'm going to loaf,
I'm not going to call it
fishing or golf or whatever.

If you raise hell,
put it down quickly or you'll get burned.

※

If you have loved and lost,
you're about even.

The trouble with life is that there are
no breaks and no time-outs.

If you're bald,
can you have a bad toupee day?

※

If the hairs on are head are numbered,
as the Bible says,
does God make bald-headed people
so He can take a day off?

No life is an easy life.

If only we could locate the fish
but also make them bite,
we wouldn't have to lie too much.

⁂

Why don't you get a discount at the barber shop
if you are mostly bald?
(I guess the barber doesn't want you to feel bad.)

Once I used my youth as an excuse,
but now I can use my old age.

I didn't want the world to stop.
I just wanted it to slow down.

⁂

Which is it?
The dumber we get, the smarter we are?
Or
the smarter we are, the dumber we get?

Do we get any points for being mixed up?

If Socrates got into trouble for
asking too many questions,
we're in trouble for not asking enough.

⁂

Friendship is the art of self-forgetfulness.

The one-track mind should jump
the track once in a while.

When I think of all the great people
who have gone before us,
I hope we haven't exhausted the supply.

☙

When people invite you into their lives,
be on your best behavior.

If happiness was once ours,
why should we think that
it will not be ours again?

When I was young, I thought
I was preparing for life, and now that
I'm old, I find that youth was not preparation
but one of the best times of my life.

☙

They say that God is slow to anger.
I surely hope so.

The Bible says that God repented
that He had made man.
I know a lot of women who would agree.

Don't ask if something will make
a difference in 100 years.
Ask if it will make a difference now.

☙

I did postgraduate work in the
University of Confusion.

I could get my act together
if I knew which act it was.

If there are a lot of thing worse than death,
name one.

☙

Can I get a leave of absence?

How can you get it together
when you're falling apart?

I applied to the University of Common Sense,
but I was turned down.

☙

If all the world's a stage,
I think I've been upstaged.

Life, at times, seems to be going up a down escalator.

If you think there's nothing wrong
with human nature,
you haven't been paying attention.

☙

If an expert is one who knows
more and more about less and less,
what do you call one who knows
less and less about more and more?

If someone asks you if you are a success,
change the subject real fast.

It isn't as easy as you would think,
introducing yourself to yourself.

☙

Spirituality is no respecter of religion.

If I wanted to tell someone off,
I wouldn't call it assertiveness training.

The reason we have second thoughts is
that we didn't think through the first one.

☙

To live the simple life is complicated.

The greatest failure of humankind is
violence in any form.

I've done modern.
It's the pits.
That goes for post-modern.

ଔ

We have only hints to the meaning of life,
and it doesn't take a genius to find them.

I wonder about multiple personality disorder.
I think I've got it.

Even a holy kiss can be construed as sexual harassment.

ଔ

When it comes to living,
there are no quick studies.

I was road kill on the information superhighway.

When life is thought of as competition,
you have to spend a lot of time keeping score.

ଔ

Socialism must be the have-nots
having had it with the haves.

To give up on democracy
is to give up on ourselves.

Don't stand too close to the cash register,
or the drawer will hit you in the stomach.

☙

If I had my life to live over,
I would probably do the same things or worse.

Once you're on the love boat,
don't abandon ship.

Tell them I didn't double-click.

☙

How many times should you tell your beloved
that you love him/her?
Say it until every glance says it for you.

All things lead to the profound,
and from the profound to mystery.

Shopkeepers of the world, unite!
You have nothing to lose but your confinement.

☙

I heard about a professor who published and perished.
(He got bad reviews.)

There's randomness in the universe
that makes us all gamblers.

It's amazing what they can do with the human heart,
except mend it when it's broken.

☙

In the afterlife, if they tell me I have to
work weekends and holidays,
I'll know exactly where I went.

Most things are taken personally.
How could it be otherwise?

Discovering people's hidden gifts
is like finding flowers in a secret garden.

☙

Memorial Day is about one thing—sacrifice.

Life allows us no retakes.

If life hasn't humbled you yet, it will.

☙

Be sure your loves outnumber your hates.

Time moves forward, whether or not we do.

I like nice people, even if they're just acting.

☙

If your big dreams don't come true,
dream little ones that will.

Though the world may be wrong,
you be right.

The rich and famous seem to associate with
those they feel are worthy of them,
and leave the rest of us alone.

☙

In America, we should strive for a
level playing field
without giving away the game by default.

When it comes to belief in God,
it takes more faith not to believe
than it does to believe.

Suppose prayer is God getting what
He wants from you, and not vice versa.

☙

One of America's sins is that it
condemns smallness when most
accomplishments are small.

It's not the theory, it's the practice.

The problem with the new era is that
we don't have new people to go with it.

☯

Ask not about one's definites
but about one's indefinites.

It doesn't matter where life's journey takes you,
as long as love finds you along the way.

When I found out that I didn't have to be
rich and famous,
I began to relax and enjoy my life.

☯

Take no day for granted.

Democracy is the ability to govern ourselves.

You can't take a walk from life.

☯

I knew it was going to be a wonderful day
when I was awakened by a kiss.

When it comes to politics and religion,
most people take them personally.
(How else?)

Even if we make a fad of spirituality,
the soul would still yearn for God.

∞

Know the difference between fad and reform.

There is a difference between arrogance and pluck.
(Though at times they look alike)

Life's direction is always forward,
regardless of the temptation to think otherwise.

∞

Don't just stop and smell the roses.
Plant a garden of roses for those coming
behind you.

Life's finals are given by you-know-who.

Why does life keep us from getting
what we think we really want?
(It must know something we don't.)

∞

When the natural disappoints us—and it will—
we have to turn to the supernatural.

Our treasures in heaven will not suffice
as collateral at the bank.
Oh, well, at least they can't be taxed, either.

As the world gets crazier, we must get saner.

☞

Two of the most wonderful words
in the English language are "No problem."

Every time I get ready to really live,
something happens until
I figure out that the happening was really living.

The church is not the main avenue of God's
working. The world is, and the church
celebrates what God is doing in the world.
(Read the Bible.)

☞

The only certainty is the search for certainty.

Belief in the absolute does not have to be
irrational; it has to be super-rational.

On God's existence: Reason says it doesn't know.
The heart yearns and hopes it's so.
The soul says yes a thousand times ten thousand.

☞

If the secret of life is not love,
what would you suggest?

You need imagination just as much
in the real world as you do in the
world of make believe.

Why is it when the economy heats up,
I'm always stone-cold broke?

※

To avoid edginess, don't live on the edge.

Do your bills fall into two categories:
past due and way past due?

If the trend continues to make life easier,
it's going to be real hard.

※

To be college educated and life educated
ought to be the same thing or thereabouts.

One person complained that life was too daily.

The one consolation in getting bald
is that you don't have to carry a comb with you.

※

Do you know of any college that gives
a degree in confusion?
Do they offer any graduate work?

I think I could get my act together
if I could just remember which act I'm in.
(It would help also to have the script.)

I don't understand all these tattoos. Do yoos?

ଔ

As I get older, I find that I am taking more
leaves of absent-mindedness.

Some people think that telling it
like it is guarantees truthfulness,
but isn't it possible to exaggerate
even then?

With what has happened to some people in the world,
you can understand why they don't mind leaving it.

ଔ

It's hard enough living with another person,
but that's easy compared to living with your self.

If you met your self on a plane,
would you want to sit next to your self?

Where did we get the idea that we have to be
happy all the time?

☯

I don't have trouble with second thoughts.
I do have trouble with third, fourth,
and fifth thoughts.
(Would you believe, even sixth or more?)

Philosophy is confusion at the highest level.

I love a simple gift, but what would
a complicated gift look like?
(I know. It's my smart phone.)

☯

No good or bad situation lasts forever.

In human affairs, we seem to be either talking
about reform or trying to instigate it.
(That should tell us something about human nature!)

You can't change human nature with slogans.
(In fact, you may not be able to change it at all.)

☯

Many have the mistaken idea
that they can avoid commitments.

I think I'll be a conservative
because they seem to have more answers.

Original sin inflicts institutions
as well as individuals
except in institutions, it's compounded.

☙

Sometimes I don't always love life,
but I don't tell anybody.

Everything depends on your love of life.

Some evils just lie there festering
with no cure in sight.

☙

Since God hasn't given us many answers
about what in the world we're doing here,
we have to live by faith.

If your nose slips from the grindstone,
don't worry.
At least your teeth will get sharpened.

A great part of America's history is
its attempt to deal with the limits
and dilemmas of freedom.

☙

Make no concessions to old age.
(Well, maybe a few.)

Don't worry about the status quo.
It never lasts.

When generalizing, be careful!

☙

Never believe you have lived beyond your age.
Many in old age feel they have lived
beyond their time, and
that is an avoidable tragedy.

You can't have a better world
without first bettering human beings.

Be sure that the light at the end of the tunnel
is not a reflection of your flashlight.

☙

Boredom is a form of selfishness.

What comes after post-modern,
post-post-modern?

Instead of striving to be happy yourself,
try being happy for someone else.

ɞ

When you boil something down,
there's not much left.

Education is a wonderful thing,
even if it doesn't end with a degree.

Exaggeration is good for humor,
but it plays havoc with the truth.

ɞ

Why does my face look so old,
when my heart feels so young?

Assuming will get you into
more trouble than asking.

Nature can play tricks on us.
(If you don't believe it, look in the mirror!)

ɞ

When it comes to reading life,
a lot of us are functionally illiterate.

The joy of every helpful discovery
for humankind is tempered by the
possibility of its misuse.

Life's uncertain journey would be
difficult indeed without the
steadying hand of a friend.

☯

You may not be able to stop progress,
but you can surely slow it down.

Since everything is becoming
entertainment, we'd better take
acting, singing, and dancing lessons.

Nothing is accomplished without discipline.
(inner and outer)

☯

I could have lived a happy life,
but the world kept interrupting.

Do you think they could put a branch of
the jet propulsion laboratory at Pasadena
in my house, so I can get up and out
in the morning?

You can preach ultimates,
but you can't practice them.

☙

Sometimes people's exuberance gets me down.

A lot of people are trying to live on
the leftovers of life's banquet.

Some people speak of being filled
as if there are reservoirs within,
but if there are, they surely have a lot of leaks.

☙

Bigger is better?
It ain't necessarily so.

You don't find self-fulfillment
in trying to fulfill the self.
You find it in fulfilling things
other than self.

Knowing the damage
they *could* do,
most people are wonderful.

☙

The world has been damaged
by misplaced enthusiasm.

We need a 12-step program
to curb us from our addiction
to consumerism.

Change may not take care of everything,
but it surely affects everything.

☯

As if we didn't have enough to worry about,
road rage has been added to the list.

Banish the word *read* as a noun.

The Holy Land is the unholy land.

☯

I'm trying to make a human being
of myself with what nature gave me.

The mark of an educated person
is his/her ongoing learning.

One thing we must not do in our old age
is to believe we have lived past our time.

☯

A real Christian works havoc with our society
just as Jesus did in His.

It's too bad editorial writers have to
write on a regular basis.
Most of them don't have that much to say.

For all the money spent on politics,
somebody is getting gypped.
(I think it's us.)

☙

I wish we could find the violence gene
in the human species
and do some genetic engineering on it.

If you find that your marriage
wasn't made in heaven,
Be sure it wasn't made in hell, either.

A "man of sorrows and acquainted with grief"
would be given Prozac today.

☙

Most people make themselves
their favorite charities.

Try having a good life,
and happiness will follow.

Why doesn't every country join NATO,
so there would be no one left to fight?

༄

Two of religion's holds on humankind
are mystery and guilt.

If changes aren't made in our politics,
I'm going to die laughing.

Some institutions are being kept alive
by artificial means, and they need to
be unplugged from their life support.

༄

The older I get,
the funnier and sadder life gets.

To read life, you need more than glasses.

The prophets were God's whistleblowers.

༄

A double whine is when you're
whining out of both sides of your mouth.

When someone tells me to get real,
I think "Really?"

I like down-to-earth people but not too earthy.

༄

Turn to God with thanksgiving
in trouble-free times, and in
troubled times, turn to God
for strength to endure.

Whatever you do, don't wrinkle my papers.

What's happening to the main-line churches
is God's down-sizing.

℘

There are no career changes from being human.

Reformers would succeed only if
they could reform human nature.

One reason we have trouble understanding
Christianity is that we can't conceive of a religion
that demands nothing but faith,
yet asks for everything.

℘

Do you think astronauts consider
themselves spaced-out?

I wonder about God calling
this person or that person.
I thought God called all of us.
(He did. We weren't listening.)

Don't worry.
You'll never be bad enough to break
your prayer chain.

☯

Some people don't need to fall off the deep end.
They fell off a long time ago.

The higher you rise in prominence,
the farther you can fall in disgrace.

"When the cat's away, the mice will play"
says more about human nature
than it does about animal nature.

☯

If you had it all, it would be too much.

Nothing reveals our character more
than how we make and use money.

I'm thinking about moving to a place
in the USA where there has been
absolutely no progress.

☯

Expect people to make fools of themselves
and for us to join in sometimes.

"Sir" and "Ma-am" are two words that should
never disappear from the English language.

If you're off the wall, find a nail to hang on to,
and they'll think you're redecorating.

&

When we are old, we spend as much time
in graveyards as we do in backyards.

Don't think there aren't secular sins
as well as religious sins.
(In fact, I think they're the same.)

Aren't you absolutely astounded at time
by your own brilliance and
your own foolishness?

&

When I was young, I could endure
almost anything as long as it was
during summer vacation.

OK, so you didn't have anything to do
with slavery, but did you take a stand
against racism?

Don't think for a moment that a
secular society can do away with sin.

☯

When do we stop doing things for our children?

Don't you wish we could add
an honesty amendment to the Constitution?

Time and tide wait for no one.
They can drown you, too.

☯

As we get older, nostalgia becomes a
compensation for neuralgia.

To tell the naked truth is lewd.
Can't you dress it up a little?

Declare yourself a success
and then get on to more important things.

☯

The secret to a long marriage is
not being able to figure out when to leave.

If you think public schools are confused
on the place of religion,
just look at the churches.

Because the Bible says the poor will
always be with us,
the rich think they're off the hook.

☙

The theory of teaching can never be
as exciting as teaching.

Success, like happiness, does not
come as an end in itself.

Can you imagine them making
prayer a political issue?
That's like trying to legislate air.

☙

Sex is one of the most powerful forces
in life, but without moral restraints,
it leads to personal and societal breakdown.

The self-fulfillment philosophy
is not very fulfilling.

In school, history classes never came up
to the present. It took me years
to figure out what was happening now.

☙

In my opinion, it takes more faith
to believe that the universe just happened
than to believe it was created with a purpose.

Every married couple should regularly
stand before the altar and repeat,
"I love you more than I possibly can say."
(And mean it.)

The law has a hard time when its meets prejudice.

☯

I'm not forgetful. I'm distracted.

Happiness comes when it's not sought
as an end in itself.

Where the action is in today's society
is the last place you want to be.

☯

Worship service to some is like a
formal sit-down dinner, while,
for others, it's more like a picnic.

We want to be celebrities until
we learn there is no privacy.

It's funny that a lot of people
who love money don't have any,
and some who have a lot come to hate it.

⁂

The only arms that should be taken up
against a democracy
are the ones used at the ballot box.

If you want a great life, get a great vision.

To believe in God is not enough.
You have to act like you believe.
(I'm not talking about perfectionism, either.)

⁂

They say we spend a third of our lives
asleep. I think that's a little short
for some of the people I know.

A child's greatest fear is abandonment.
So is an adult's.

It's tragic to call just some of the places on
Earth holy, when all places have
the potential of being holy.

⁂

The computer age just doesn't compute.
It hasn't taught me the secrets of the universe.

Most people's hidden agendas should remain so.

The information revolution gave me
the wrong information.

&

I prefer to be out of shape than bent out of shape.

I don't envy God's job.

With all the talk of rights,
doesn't the community have rights, too?

&

Make sure your rights don't conflict
with society's rights.

Death is unconditional surrender.

Declare war on despair and make peace with regrets.

&

Peace treaties with life have to be
constantly renegotiated.

I would have done a lot of wonderful
things in life if I hadn't had to work.

Human beings are animals with consciences.
That's our glory and our misery.

⁂

Why is it when we've had a good life,
we worry that it should have been better?

I can't retire because I don't have the
money or the energy.

It takes more faith to believe in nothing
than it does to believe in something.

⁂

In our fallen world, I'm constantly
amazed at how well we do.

When you're between a rock and a hard place,
don't forget your hammer and chisel.

We never pay in full our debt to society.

⁂

Hatred is no respecter of race or religion,
or anything else, for that matter.

Some people don't want to solve problems;
they just want to fuss at them.

Science explores mystery while religion exalts it.

☯

Our emotions determine
our philosophy of life, or lack of it.

Pay attention to what people do
more than what they say.

Human behavior is, at times, as baffling
to those who study it as to those who don't.

☯

If a woman's work is never done,
you can bet a man's work is never done, either.
(That's what "Honey do" lists are for.)

It's a great world as worlds go.

We didn't ask to come here.
We just kind of showed up.

☯

If we turn over everything to God,
He will turn it back to us and say
He'll help us through it.

I took a new lease on life,
but I couldn't make the payments.

You're showing your age when you
begin to say, "It used to be…" or
"We always did it this way."

☙

I wanted to reflect on my life,
but I couldn't get it to slow down.

Perhaps it takes more character
to endure riches than it does poverty.

Love may not have been born
on that first Christmas Day,
but it surely got its biggest boost.

☙

We are born in mystery,
live in mystery, and die in mystery.

Why do answers always lead to more questions?

I had a wonderful life.
I just didn't realize it at the time.

☙

How wonderful to have your life
accompanied by great music,
great ideas, and a great love.

Someone's faith may be as deep as yours,
but they may draw their inspiration
from a different source.

There's a price to pay when you're right
as well as when you're wrong.

☯

Great principles focus our minds
until our experiences can authenticate them.

"The Good Lord's willing and the creek don't rise"
just about covers it.

True religion is not magic.

☯

It took a long time for me to realize
that people without a Southern accent
could be nice.

At times, it looks like the barbarians
are not only at the gates;
they have crashed through them.

When I finally got back to my fighting weight,
I didn't want to fight anymore.

☯

If Mozart composed minuets at five,
and symphonies at nine,
what's wrong with my grandson?

The older we get, the richer we get,
at least in memories.

You can make people miserable,
but it's almost impossible to make them happy.

☯

One consolation to global warming—
no Ice Age.

We never stop trying to succeed,
even in retirement.

We usually find an outlook
that matches our temperament.

☯

We are captivated by stories
because we keep looking to find
ourselves in them.

Just when you think you've heard it all,
you ain't heard nothin' yet.

Live in wonderment.

☯

A shoestring budget usually gets knotted up.

It took me a while to learn that brashness
doesn't always come with a Northern accent.

I believe in second chances. In fact,
I believe in as many chances as is necessary.

☯

When you're on a roll, be sure it's not downhill.

They said, "Go for it." I did but I couldn't find it.

Let the tidal wave of thanksgiving
drown the sorrows and tragedies of life.

☯

Humans are like polls in one respect.
There's a big margin of error.

There are no boring lives.
There are lives that have not discovered
how interesting they are and
how interesting the world is.

Just when you think you have the answer,
a new question pops up.

☙

Prayer is not so much getting God
to do what we want as
God getting us to do what He wants.

The longer I live, the deeper the mystery.

Some say we learn most from our failures,
but who wants to learn that much.
(That's why they call it a hard lesson.)

☙

I don't like uncritical conservatism
any more than I like uncritical liberalism.

I knew I'd retire one day;
I just didn't know I'd get old, too.

When all good things come to an end,
just keep adding good things.

☙

Academics can't have a good laugh
until they have discussed the philosophy of humor.

Have you noticed that the weather
doesn't pay much attention to the equinoxes?

Some people love deeply, but
they have a funny way of showing it.

ଘ

It's not enough to tell the truth.
You have to figure out how to tell it.

Never mind how we got here.
The real question is what are we going to do here?

I've always tried to avoid fame and fortune,
and so far, I've succeeded.

ଘ

Just accept the fact that
life is never completely fulfilled.

I pray that at the end of my life,
I will be able to say,
"It was all worth it."

Suppose the times aren't worth keeping up with?

ଘ

The past should be honored, not worshipped.

Tradition doesn't have to mean
"stuck in the past." It can be a living thing.

We grow up in love's riches when
we are deep in our mother's heart.

☙

I just heard on the radio Tom T. Hall singing
"Old Dogs, Children, and Watermelon Wine."
It means more to me now than it did in
1972 when it first came out.

There are truths that are certain,
but our hold on them is uncertain.

In the sweep of history,
don't get thrown out with the trash.

☙

God is too large an idea for science
with its limited methodology.

I've been called ahead of my time and
behind the times, but all I'm trying to do
is stay even with the times.

I think I could keep up with the times
if I could just tell what time it is.

※

Civilization is our feeble attempt
to control the uncontrollable.
(Mother Nature)

A leader can't be a leader
unless someone follows.

Most of us are mere observers of history
and not makers of history, but either way,
what a show!

※

I wanted to make something of myself,
but I found that it depended as much
on others as it did on me.

The greatest gift we humans possess
is our capacity for joy.

The reason the ACLU looks silly at times
is because it tries to make freedom an absolute.

※

The law runs into trouble when it
tries to encompass absolutes.

Remember it is Christ's church that
is finest and foremost, and ours is
only a distant second.

Forgive me, Lord, if I should ever think
that I could live a life immune from sorrow.

☯

Sometimes I feel, for a split second,
that I lived in another time and in another life.

At Christmas, we have a hanging of the greens,
but afterward, we should have an
un-hanging of the greens.

Make your declining years your aspiring years.
(for God, that is)

☯

Do you know what doctor's handwriting is?
Illegible. *(My handwriting is so bad, some
thought I should start practicing medicine at once.)*

In the spiritual life, retreating is advancing.

Try to know God in this life,
lest you'll be an embarrassment
on the Day of Judgment to be
introduced for the first time.

Faith or religion is part truth,
part poetry, and part fiction.
Two out of three ain't bad.

I hope the quality of education is not
in direct proportion to the size
of the diploma.

If we understood life,
all the wonder would be taken away.

∞

Since the tensions of life won't go away,
we've got to work on our elasticity.

We usually judge out of context.

In America, we have the separation
of church and state but not of
business and state.

∞

Save pining for conifers.

Thank goodness to be a player in life
doesn't depend on athletic ability.

To live is to be unfulfilled; it is the soil of growth.

☙

Whenever there is mystery,
can religion be far behind?
(Or science, for that matter)

Some people want their religion to be magic
and their ministers to be magicians.

Since so many people want to come to America,
and I've been here all along,
I saved myself a lot of trouble.

☙

God put enough goodness in the world
to make us believers,
and enough evil in the world
to make us doubters,
so why go through life
vacillating between the two?

Givings and Misgivings would make
a good book title.

If it's not one thing, it's another.
Well, of course!

☙

Ideals, by their very nature,
are unattainable,
and those who think they are,
are delusional.

Being in denial is not always bad,
except when it pertains to
setting ourselves free.

I thought music and I were on
speaking terms, but lately I'm not so sure.

☯

In a democracy, we should always strive
for equality, but when we fail, let us
fall back on the solid belief that
we are as good as anyone, but no better.

Don't regret that you didn't do a big thing.
Do a lot of little things, and they will
amount to something big.

It all boils down to a matter of time,
and money, or both.

☯

The more you think about life,
the more of life there is to think about.

If I keep studying, I might become a scholar,
and if my manners improved, I could
add to that "a gentleman."

Do more transforming than conforming.

☯

If this is all there is, make it more than it is.

The greatest compliment is
to be invited into someone's life.

Solid ground is not as solid as we thought.

☯

Adolescents don't rebel;
they conform to their peers.

History should teach us
that people of the past were just like us.

When all else fails, we could put on
some old clothes and shave our heads
and become gurus.

☯

Those who live in the basement
shouldn't complain about windows.

Remember you're on a first-name basis with God.

Be controversial rather than inconsequential.

※

When you're behind, rally.

A moral victory is not everything.
It is the only thing.

Be very careful in thinking that
another's faith is not as fervent as yours.

※

The "gospel" means "good news"
but it often comes with bad news.

The sermon should not be a jaw breaker
but a joy maker.

Palm Sunday depended on humans.
Easter Sunday depended on God.

※

Never leave the land of awe.

You have to be sane to be executed,
but society doesn't.

I should have been a great man,
for I surely had a great mother.

☙

You may lose your faith if you don't
practice it religiously.

I was seduced by Sophia.

Just say that I had a long-time
love affair with great ideas.

☙

I would live in the moment
but I'm too busy.

From the tyranny of the clock,
Good Lord deliver us.

Don't let your little regrets
crowd out your big regrets.

☙

If something like 98 percent
of Americans believe in God,
why isn't this a better country?

Life is always unfinished business.

You really know you're retired,
when you wake up in the morning
with no reason to get out of bed.

☙

Learn to live three days at a time —
yesterday, today, and tomorrow.

You can almost bank on it.
What the world thinks is important
is not what God thinks is important.

A champion loses with a lot of grace
but wins with a lot more.

☙

The magic of life isn't always
at the beginning. It can be in the middle
or at the end.

An important consideration is not
that we say too much or too little,
but when to speak and when to remain silent.

The understanding of life is the living of it.

☙

There is an incalculable difference
between failing and being a failure.

Thank goodness there is such a thing
as poetic license for life.

Old age is a phase of life we're not
going to live through.

☙

We can't live old age down, so we have to live it up.

Why is life almost over
when we feel we're just getting started?

I wanted to be somebody,
but I couldn't figure out which somebody to be.

☙

The trouble with living a dream
is that you have to wake up.

Don't make everything a problem!

You can expect violence from people in a
primitive stage of spiritual development.

☙

I'm counting on God's mercy,
but I'm also counting on His sense of humor.

I haven't recognized anything since
Ozzie & Harriet.

Have you noticed that people don't
notice something until it happens to them?

⁂

Stop trying to be somebody
when you're already somebody.

Right makes right, not might.

A sermon should not try to prove God
but to improve us.

⁂

We must teach our children not
to be discouraged by the contradictions of life.

I hate to see women imitating the
competitive world of men. It's the
least attractive thing about them.

Let life's discontents be sources of growth,
not platforms for complaint.

⁂

Why are towel dispensers
so high on the wall that the
water runs down your arms?

One serious conflict between
religion and science is the
significance and insignificance
of humans.

I'd rather be historically correct
than politically correct.

⁘

We used to call nature God,
but now we call it Mother Nature.
At least we've kept it in the family!

Who but God could love all humans
all of the time?

Those who live in the realm of appreciation
use the word "wonderful" a lot.

⁘

Degrees give the false impression
that one's education has been completed.

One reason we don't feel at home in the world
is that we're not here long enough.

If there is one group that needs to improve
its gene pool, it's the Anglo-Saxons.

℘

Why do some people believe the unbelievable?

You can go broke slowly or quickly,
but either way, you'll be broke.

Christianity is often condemned for the
way it treats unbelievers.

℘

If God has a sense of humor,
I think I'll make it.

You can't cover over an unhappy life
by running around the woods,
playing revolutionary soldier.

Whatever humans build inevitably falls into ruins.

℘

"Quality time" is often an excuse for
not spending "quantity time."

You may not be in business for your health,
but, believe me, no health, no business.

If you try to make life a win-win situation,
you not only will be disappointed,
but you won't learn anything.

⽯

I've had enough experience with the
human world not to be too impressed.
Now the world of nature:
Ah, that's another matter!

One thing this electronic information
revolution has not improved is our character.

The mind is like the spirit; it's always hungry.

⽯

When you hold a baby, you hold a miracle.

What's the opposite of "up and coming"?
"Down and going," I suppose.

You can be dishonorably discharged for
disgracing the uniform; too bad you can't be
dishonorably discharged from the
human race for disgracing humanity.
(Or maybe that's what hell is for.)

⽯

If we all lived together, it would be
too crowded, but we ought to be
able to get along, at least.

I don't know about "better late than never."
What if lateness leads to never?

ꝏ

What's wrong with marrying
for love AND money?

The most frightening words in a marriage
are those said by one to the other,
"We need to talk."

Two of the happiest words are
"No charge." *(Or "No problem.")*

ꝏ

Why is something considered "on sale"
when it's been "for sale" all along?

They call me a bi-vocational minister.
Doesn't that sound indecent to you?

There is a lot of difference
between moving to the right and being right.

ꝏ

Sometimes I'm liberal,
sometimes conservative,
sometimes reactionary,
and sometimes moderate.
So, what does that make me?
I guess I'm just mixed up.

If people are on drugs
because they can't deal with life,
they have more than a drug problem.

We ministers in small churches
have failed a little,
but the ministers in mega-churches
have failed a lot.

☯

Telling it like it is doesn't ensure truthfulness.
People lie.

People say we're falling apart,
but as I read history, it seems that
every society has felt that way.

On Judgment Day,
are you going to say you got more than you gave?

☯

Since all other civilizations have fallen,
why do we think ours will be the exception?
(Arrogance, I guess.)

Life costs so much.
Do you think it will ever go on sale?

Small retail businesses are disappearing.
That's sad because they were
the only places that knew me.

⊗

Have you ever noticed that your freedom
is bumping into other people's freedom?

Each 4th of July, every American
should read the
Declaration of Independence and
the Constitution.
*(Except lawyers and judges
should read them every day.)*

Have you ever noticed the expressions
on a woman's face when she's shopping?

⊗

Some say that television and movies have
ruined young people.
(What a relief! I thought we had done that.)

Men are put on Earth for one purpose
and one purpose only—to make women happy.

Practice makes perfect,
but nobody is perfect,
so should we keep practicing or give up?

൞

If you want to have an inferiority complex,
study astronomy.
(In lieu of that, look at the sky on a starry night.)

People talk about unwinding
like they're some kind of spring.
Boing!

Perhaps the best thing we can leave
our children is a future.

൞

God bless America. He's already done that.
Now, we have to help Him with the other countries.

If someone tells you the great days are in the past,
you tell them the great days are just beginning
because you are in them.

A great love is life's masterpiece.

൞

Ask God to turn your curses into blessings.

The human parade has never been rained out.
(Thank goodness!)

A new friend of mine told me
I had gaps in my education.
After knowing me for a while,
he said my gaps were more like canyons.

☙

I guess I've had about as much freedom
as I could handle.

Old age must have some compensations
for the falling apart process.
(Can you think of any?)

The church is not the main arena of
God's activity; the world is.

☙

A southern accent is music without notes.

Some people need more practice at being human.

God didn't give Himself for the church.
He gave Himself for the world.

☙

When you give it your best shot,
make sure your aim is good.

Some listen to the music of the spheres
while others are tone deaf.

Do you know why we went into space?
There was nowhere else to go but up.

☙

When it rains, it pours.
Do what Noah did. Build a big boat.

When a situation is going from bad to worse,
RUN!

Many would seize the day
if they knew where the handle is.

☙

Wouldn't you like to see banks have an
interest war to really compete?

If your life is not a great adventure,
why isn't it?

We shouldn't call it retirement;
we should call it advancement.

☙

If you're not the hero in your own life,
who would you suggest?

Have you asked yourself enough questions?

Moses was a moralist. You'd better believe it.

❦

Try to live a life of quiet inspiration.

Did you ever consider the fine line
between taking the Lord's name in vain
and praying?

When society falls apart, do we try to put
it back together or just pick up the pieces?

❦

Of all the planning I did in my life,
I forgot to plan for old age.
(I don't mean pensions!)

When you're down, just consider
seeing it from a different perspective.

I was always planning to do something
great with my life, but it went by too fast.

❦

Professional wrestling is perfect training
for a politician. Both have to fake it.

If the world passes you by,
be grateful you were able to see it pass.

Happiness is not grab-able.
It must grab you.

&

To preach the love of God
and neighbor is our highest calling,
not only to preach but to practice.

There is nothing like bad religion
to close the mind, and nothing like
good religion to open it.

When I was young, I had a lot of answers,
But when I became old, I forgot most of them.

&

To crowd out selfishness,
it takes a lifetime of conversions.

"To thine own self be true,"
and I ask, which self is that?

Suffer fools gladly since we're
all fools at something—and
at times everything.

❧

Life is a race between reason and mystery,
and in the end, mystery wins.

The trouble with many people who
know the difference between right and wrong
is that what they think is right is wrong,
and what they think is wrong is right.

Many times our choices are between
the least right and the least wrong.

❧

We're all hypocrites.
let's just try to be less so.

You may think that one day is not
very important, yet it is the
accumulation of days that makes a life.

I seldom get depressed, but
I often get disgusted.
That may be about the same thing.

❧

Of all the surprises in life,
my biggest one was getting old.
(I didn't think it would happen.)

Forgiveness is life's eraser.

Sometimes I whistle because I'm happy,
but most of the time
it's to keep up my courage.

⊱⊰

Write your life story with a pencil
and keep a big eraser handy.

If we live long enough,
we're all damaged goods.

Look for meanings in life
for you will not find "The Meaning."

⊱⊰

For the first time in American history,
we are beginning to question progress.

In a democracy,
the government is overthrown
at the ballot box.

I thought I was running until the votes came in,
and then I found that I was only crawling.

⊱⊰

Where does a rainbow go,
and where is that pot of gold, anyway?

If you've never rocked in a rocking chair,
you've missed out on one of life's great pleasures.

There is no room in great religions
for hate, except perhaps for that which
diminishes them.

∞

I didn't mind the work; it was the aggravation.

Marriage is a two-way street;
the trick is not to make it a one-way street.

With a stacked deck,
it's hard to play the hand you're dealt.

∞

Work to keep America from becoming
the land of the greed and
the home of the depraved.

Confronted with the immensity of the universe,
how in heaven's name could we be
anything but humble?

In life, tell them I aspired to be the court jester.

Old age kind of slips up on us.

The positive side of nature causes us to be here,
and the negative side causes us not to stay.

Where do you go to sign up for a guardian angel?

☙

We must learn to live more with not knowing
than we do with knowing.

One of the tenets of democracy is that
the majority rules, but by the looks of
American voting records, the minority rules.

We have to be careful in
putting a moral judgment on nature.

☙

The Christian faith does involve a leap of faith,
but the question is where do you take the leap?

I wanted to think outside the box,
but I couldn't open it.

Nixon taught us that we can
survive any failure, and
Clinton taught us we can
survive any embarrassment.

☙

It's very difficult for the church
to do the Christian thing.

I used to view old age like a child
does Christmas; it seems to take
forever to arrive, but it does.

I loved learning.
It was the unlearning that I hated.

☙

If youthful indiscretions can be overlooked,
why can't elderly indiscretions?

Anticipation sometimes is
greater than the thing itself.

Don't be yourself. Be nice instead.

☙

Mixing religion and politics elevates politics
too high and brings religion down too low.

We usually use an ounce of reason
to a pound of rationalization.

Gratitude will get you attitude.

☯

Divisions in the church are nothing
but a failure in love.

It's hard to live the American dream
when you know that many are living
an American nightmare.

You never get an education.
You're always being educated;
that is, if you're teachable.

☯

Put an OPEN sign in front of your mind.

I'd hate to see a self-made man.

I'm glad that life knocked me out of
thinking I was too good for menial tasks.

☯

The Lord giveth and the Lord taketh away,
but sometimes He taketh away before He giveth.

At best, life is a mixed bag.
Its meaning is not in the mixture
but in how you carry it.

Sometimes forward is backward,
and backward is forward.
The trick is to know the difference.

☯

We can learn something even from boredom.

Experience is not the best teacher
until you've had the right experiences.

More people go off the shallow end
than go off the deep end.

☯

Into every life, some rain must fall,
but does it have to come down in buckets?

Art does not give us an excuse to be unkind.
(Nor does anything else, for that matter.)

Fight cynicism with everything you've got,
and don't be afraid to call in reinforcements.

☯

Many social problems cannot be solved
by money alone, but they can't be solved
completely without it.

Ponder long and hard before you
make yourself an exception.

It took me a long time to become a liberal,
which I thought was being open-minded.

❧

Miracles are aimed at the heart, not the mind.

Can you imagine the rich needing
Affirmative Action?

If you can find it in your heart,
don't look anywhere else.

❧

Our lives are different yet how alike.

How easy a force becomes a farce!

Never underestimate a smile,
or overestimate one, either.

❧

In passing through this world,
for heaven's sake,
be on your best behavior.

We learn more from our failures
than we learn from our successes,
but don't tell the world that.

Did you ever think you would have to
go back behind the barn to smoke
where you learned to do it in the first place?

※

The past seems as uncertain as the future;
we keep reinterpreting it.

If you're up the creek without a paddle,
relax and go with the flow.

God's love is the only inexhaustible source.

※

Life needs a lot of course corrections.

If you think money is not important,
try living without any.

When you run aground,
make it your port of call.

❦

There's more than one way to skin a cat,
but don't let the Humane Society find out about it.

Is there anything more lonesome sounding
than a train whistle in the night?

Can we ever get enough of autumn?
Can we ever get enough of spring?

❦

Never be intimidated by knowledge.
Be intimidated by the lack of it.

Where there is truth, embrace it.
Where there is error, correct it.

Love and hate are both irrational.
Pray you fall on the love side of irrationality.

❦

Without God, we think we're God.

Be sure that the fire in your belly
isn't just indigestion.

If only I had a computer,
I'd have an excuse.

Now that I'm a published poet,
I think I'll become eccentric.

Deliver me from writers
but not their writings.

Dissatisfaction is framed in the human heart
not as a source of unhappiness
but as an incentive to strive.

※

When you're at sea, remember your life jacket.

The trouble with the rat race
is that you're running in bad company.

"The rest is history," they say,
but could it be anything else?

※

The trouble with rich folks is that
when people look at them,
they see only their money, not them.

Are a lot of writers neurotic
because they write,
or do they write
because they are neurotic?

Just as we can fall in love,
we can fall in hate.

ଚ

A light heart lives long,
but a heavy heart has more in it.

Customers are always right,
even when they're wrong.

Some people apologize for living a simple life,
while others would consider themselves so lucky.

ଚ

If your life is boring,
perhaps your attention span is too short.

If you can't fool Mother Nature,
who else is worth fooling?

We won't let our politicians tell us what they think.
Instead, they tell us what we think.

ଚ

I got seized by the day.

Those who try to paint life by the numbers
don't get the true picture.

Don't you long to hear someone stand up and say,
"I'm responsible."
"It's my fault."
"I'll take the blame"?

☯

It's easy to pick a fight,
but harder to pick the right one.

We know we're in trouble when we have
to schedule spontaneity.

Why is it that when I finally
understand something, it's out of date?

☯

One of life's great tasks is to have a
balanced self image, not too high or too low.

The declining years are the defining years.

We're not senior citizens.
We're seasoned citizens.

☯

The funny thing about love is
that it can break your heart,
but it can also put it back together.

Astronomers say the earth wobbles a bit,
and I know it's true, because I can feel it
every once in a while when I walk.

If we fell off the edge of the universe,
where would we land?

&

If rock bands made better music than
better fools of themselves, it would help.

Love can make you crazy,
but you can't be really sane without it, either.

Love given as a reward
inevitably leads to resentment.

&

Love given as a gift to both giver and receiver
inevitably leads to gratitude.

Get up every morning and thank God
you're not rich or famous, or both.

England has a class system, and they're proud of it.
America has a caste system,
and they're ashamed of it.

&

I think small business can compete with
big business in at least one area: bankruptcy.

Did you hear about the business that did
so poorly, it didn't even have a bottom line?

Stand close enough to life to see
its humor as well as its pathos.

☙

Faith without quirks is dead.

Where is life's safety net?

Even if life were a bed of roses,
the thorns would worry you to death.

☙

The happiest people I've found are
those who do not seem to think
about themselves all the time.

There's a lot of jibberish out there,
and we have to learn to separate
the "jibber" from the "ish."

It's a funny thing about money.
Too much can bring a lot of unhappiness,
but so can not enough money.

❧

Next to love, humor may be
life's most important ingredient.

Cultivate a sense of humor and
pray that in the end, it won't forsake you.

In a debate, don't worry which side won.
Worry whether or not truth won.

❧

Don't be a dream killer.
Be a nightmare killer.

Get back to your fighting weight.

Someone should write a book on
when good and bad things happen
to good and bad people.

❧

Apologies to Henry David Thoreau.
If one does not keep step with his fellows,
perhaps he hears the beat of a distant drummer,
or maybe he's just out of step. Period.

We shouldn't keep asking children
what they want to be when they grow up,
lest we diminish their childhood.

The only thing I can figure out
is that when opportunity knocked,
I was in the shower.

☙

"Forever and a day." Can you
believe someone wants to add a day to forever?

There are no second chances in life;
there are thousands of chances.

Be sure you know the difference
between what goes without saying
and what needs to be said.

☙

God starts with the mundane and
elevates it to the sublime.
(Look at us.)

God must have infinite patience.
We're still here, aren't we?

The declining years are the refining years.

☙

The bad thing about winter and summer
is that they last too long.

I love life! *(Most of the time)*

At least, be a foot soldier in the battle of life.

☙

Hasn't everyone wondered how
we happened to be here, and why?

If colleges and universities don't do a better job,
we're going to have to refer to them as
lower education.

Life has no exchange policy.

☙

Did you know about the person who was
so busy she couldn't get anything done?

If you don't believe very much,
preach short sermons.

Love life and it will love you back.

☙

Short-sightedness is not a
good condition for visionaries.

I wish that people would get as excited about
God as they do about money.

You know you're getting old
when you're little vices aren't fun anymore.

&

Certainty was never one of life's long suits.

Don't hold your own counsel until you
have consulted the counsel of others.

There's nothing wrong with
self-fulfilling prophesies.

&

Life doesn't turn out the way we expected,
but what does turn out can be
pretty wonderful.

They say that if you want to get something done,
go to a busy person.
I did, but I couldn't get an appointment.

How can I be old when I was young all my life?

&

Life would be a lot better
if rules didn't have exceptions.

Before you label yourself,
remember that problems
do not come with labels.

The only thing you should do for a bias
is to cut on it.

☯

The best way to be objective is to
watch out for your biases.

Don't hide your prejudice behind ideology.

Two things have not diminished with age:
love of God and love of country.

☯

Every person has lived an interesting story
if only we could hear it.

Life is always approximate.

Have you noticed that the
new Democrats look like old Republicans?

☯

I can't quite understand all this talk about
"family values." Where I came from,
we never left them.

I would have a good outlook on life
if life had a good outlook on me.

One reason I hate to die is that
I want to see how everything turns out.

&

Human nature contradicts every
theory we have of it.

It's too bad we can't demonstrate against aging.

I wanted to be a mover and a shaker,
but I shook more than I moved.

&

Life is a perpetual on-the-job training.

Life does not allow even one day off.

Life is change.
How original is that?

&

You can take a lot of challenges
if you're not afraid of losing.

Being an exception to every rule
brings on a lot of headaches.

You don't have to be smart to teach,
but it helps.

☙

When we forget that we are seriously flawed,
we lose the essential human perspective.

The only one who should be able to
intimidate us is God Almighty.

Life defies theories.

☙

A lot of people really think that
"out of mind" is really "out of sight."

If we had stayed in church,
we never would have gotten away
from family values.

Love the past, but love the future more.

☙

The more I live, the more
I appreciate the time I have left,
however long or short that may be.

Do obligations have term limits?

Adversity can teach us valuable lessons, or not.

☙

Nothing is more pitiful than an aging hippie.

Life seems to get more precious
in proportion to the time we have left.

They said someone was a wannabe.
My God, aren't we all?

☙

Some things just fade away.

What impresses us reveals our character.

When we compare what we do know
and what we don't know.
What we do know pales in comparison.

☙

It's too bad we can't legislate
against the inevitable.

Pray that you do not come to a bitter end.

If God delights in us as we delight
in our children, then we have learned
an important attribute of God.

☯

Everyone's life is exciting
if you know where to look.

Democracy breaks down when civility does.

I spend so much time going back
to the drawing board that I
don't get anything done.

☯

Why are so many conservatives so uptight?

Sometimes I hate life,
but sometimes it hates me.

How fortunate that all our wishes
don't come true.

☯

Social consciousness is not a luxury
but a necessity.

Don't be a burden to someone's spirit.

Nature is not democratic, so we must be.

☯

Faith puts a good face on life.

Seek as if your life depended on it.
(It does.)

My life always seems to have
extenuating circumstances.

☙

Thoreau said that most men live
lives of quiet desperation,
and well some of them should.

Business was so bad one Christmas that
people were forced to think of its true meaning.

Romantics have a hard time with this world.

☙

Start out as a "has-been" and you will have
already begun mounting one of life's
greatest disappointments.

Blessings are too many to be counted,
so we have to settle for an estimate.

I made a lot of enemies,
but I never lost a real friend.
Judge Tuttle
(The same thing happened to me.)

☯

Why not suffer fools gladly? God does.

Pray that our flag at half-staff will not be
the norm for our beloved country.

Only God can say, "This way and no other."

☯

Fight fads and stick to the basics.

Is this all there is?
(Well, what did you expect?"

When it comes to life, we're never over-qualified.

☯

The road of gratitude is paved with joy.

Is there a place that hasn't made too
much progress? I think I'll move there.

Sometimes the only choice is on which
evil we will take sides.

☯

I can't figure out whether or not
I'm pre-computer or post-computer.

If may be difficult to make someone happy,
but it isn't difficult to make someone miserable.

The music of life has to be played by ear.

৪০

Just tell them I was an opportunist
devoid of opportunities.

Sorry, Vince Lombardi.
Winning is not the only thing,
since in the end we lose.

We don't really want to understand life
completely lest all wonder would be gone.

৪০

I wanted to make something of myself
but the makings were slim.

Don't worry about maintaining the status quo.
It can't be done.

The test of whether or not we have risen
above our animal nature is to
subdue violence.

৪০

There is nothing like getting older
to change your perspective.

I told my banker that my finances
were having a slight correction.
He didn't buy it.

I must admit at times to world weariness.
(WW, that is.)

☙

A lot of politicians could become statesmen
if the people would let them.

Life kinda mixed me up.

When does the right to know
become the right to know too much?

☙

The world within us is as dazzling
as the world without *(maybe more so)*.

With old age comes the lessening
of the urge to straighten everyone out.

When it comes time to draw a line in the sand,
be sure there is enough sand.

☙

Can you name a time when the world
wasn't going to the dogs?
Or to hell in a hand basket?

Happiness is never made.
It is shared.

All gold is fool's gold.

&

You don't think people are snooty
if you're one of the snoots.

I don't need my memory refreshed.
I need it reconstructed.

Two happinesses are better than one.

&

Oliver Wendell Holmes said that
taxes are what we pay for civilization,
but I think we're getting gypped.

God never falls out of love with us.
(I can't say as much for humans.)

To be happy, find happy people,
and add your happiness to theirs.

❦

I'm basking in grandparenthood.

Get the dread out.

Rich is as rich does.

❦

A religious war should be a contradiction in terms.

How often we repress the bad moments and remember the good ones.
(Ain't psychology wonderful?)

My best psychological trick is repression, second only to denial.

❦

The Sun is not a renewable resource.

Sometimes I think Mother Nature is not an environmentalist.
(Did you see the eruption the other day?)

I don't need to watch sitcoms.
I watch politics.

❦

Are defining moments in the dictionary?

There is a world of difference
between a person of the world
and a worldly person.

Our soul mate is God.
(Did you think it was anyone else?)

☯

Some people think there's a free lunch
because they can charge it.

I think I'll never get over fretting
about bigness and learn to love Walmart.

When I made my mark, it got smudged.

☯

The only horse that came in for me
was named Charlie.

Whenever I hear Frank Sinatra sing,
my whole life passes in front of me.

Who said we couldn't make it?
(I didn't.)

☯

Why not ask for whom the bell tolls?
It could be for somebody else.
(Apologies to John Donne.)

When I got rid of my clutter,
I got rid of my life.

The trouble with ecstasy is that
it's always in such short supply.
(I'm not talking about the drug.)

☙

Don't refer to a business as a "firm."
There's nothing firm about it these days.

Whenever I saw Mother Teresa,
I forgot there was such a thing as original sin.

When a corrupt totalitarian government
moves to democracy, often what you
can get is a corrupt democracy.

☙

One of our greatest benefits is
the "benefit of the doubt."
(Apply it to others and yourself carefully.)

In life, we're always in training.

Our reason is like a small boat
floating on a sea of emotion.

☞

It takes a great deal of patriotism
to confront the country's injustices
and try to do something about it.

The biggest mistake our permissive society
makes is to believe we can be value-free.

When you're feeling too important,
look up at the stars.

☞

When you're eyeball to eyeball
with loneliness,
don't be the first to blink.

Big bucks usually means big greed.

The reason I don't play the numbers game
is because I don't have my numbers.

☞

The only thing that doesn't change
is change itself.

To forgive is not to condone.

From dust we came and
to dust we shall return
leaves a lot to be desired.

☙

I'm intolerant of intolerance!
(And so should we all.)

May your death be as beautiful
as the fall,
and your rising as beautiful
as the spring.

I wonder about "world class"
for fear it might have more "world"
in it than "class."

☙

In business, the bottom line is
not my dictator, and of course,
I'm going broke.

To follow the crowd is a sure sign
of not knowing where you're going.

The far left and the far right
are likely to meet.
(It's called paranoia.)

☙

It takes more than diversity
to improve society.

You know you're getting old
when you don't recognize
the young singers and movie stars.

It's amazing that at a time of
Moral laxity, there is such a
Hunger for God!
(Maybe that's the reason.)

☯

The more people forget God,
the more they unconsciously remember Him.

Christianity gives more of a direction
to life than it does an explanation of life.

Is it more important to know where
you're going than where you've been?
(Naw.)

☯

If you can take pleasure in the little things,
your life will be endless fascination.

Dirt cheap is usually just that.

Life is the only game you're forced to play,
whether or not you know all the rules.

☯

Could you say it's all God's fault?
(He started it.)

I never knew what the devil is due,
did you?

Winter or summer,
be sure you have high humility.

☯

Most of us are not smart enough to be a
consistent conservative or liberal or
most anything else.
(So what's the deal?)

I didn't dodge the draft.
The draft dodged me.

My mother taught me that
two wrongs don't make a right.
*(But, Mama, how about one wrong
and one right canceling each other out?)*

☯

Have you noticed that we now
live in rip-off city?
(I wish I could move.)

I don't understand all these tattoos.
Do youse?

What do people mean when they say
they are spiritual but not religious?
(Does not religion involve the Spirit?)

☯

Believers should help God make
religion a blessing to the world
and not a curse.

Tell 'em I tried to get it right!
(But I was conspired against.)

My mother used to say,
"I don't know what to do or how to do."

www.ingramcontent.com/pod-product-compliance
Lightning Source LLC
Chambersburg PA
CBHW020618300426
44113CB00007B/691